Border Buddy
Ultimate Template for Borders, Corners and Cut-Outs
Scrapbooking is more fun with a

Tips & How To's

We've provided a variety of Marker Holes on each Border Buddy® to help you create those perfect corners and borders on all size scrapbook pages! Keep in mind that practice makes perfect and we want you to get the best results from your Border Buddy®. Follow the tips below and practice on scratch paper before diving in on your actual scrapbook pages.

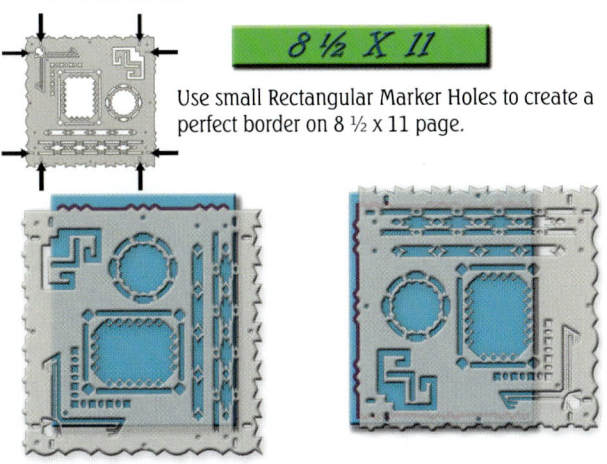

Use your Border Buddy® "this side up."

Store your Border Buddy® flat and avoid hanging.

Clean your Border Buddy® with a soft cloth.

Be creative and have fun!!

Create Perfect Borders

12 X 12

Step One	Step Two	Step Three	Step Four

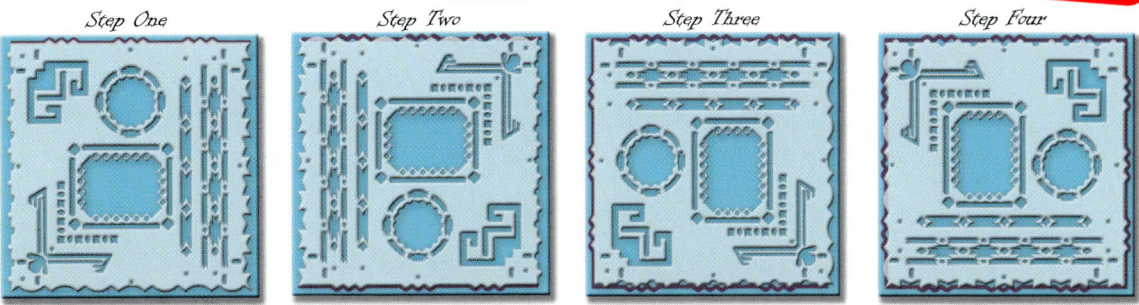

- Center Border Buddy on page about ¼" from top edge.
- Trace top line.

- Turn Border Buddy and repeat for bottom edge.
- Trace bottom line.

- Center Border Buddy between top and bottom line.
- Trace side line.

- Repeat for right side line.

8 ½ X 11

Use small Rectangular Marker Holes to create a perfect border on 8 ½ x 11 page.

- Place Border Buddy with desired edge about ¼" from top of page.
- Line up the inside edges of the Rectangular Marker Holes with the outside edges of the of the short side of the page.
- Trace edge, starting and stopping about ¼" from each side.
- Repeat for bottom line.

- Turn and center Border Buddy between drawn top and bottom lines, trace side edge.
- Repeat for other side.

Any Other Size

Use small round Center Holes in the center of each edge to center on odd size pages.

- Find the center of your page with a ruler. Mark lightly with a pencil.
- Line up Center Hole with the center of the page.
- Trace edge.
- Repeat for other edges as desired.

Corners

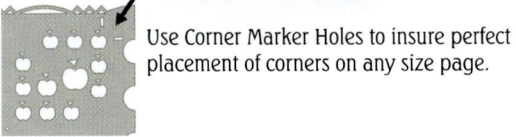

Use Corner Marker Holes to insure perfect placement of corners on any size page.

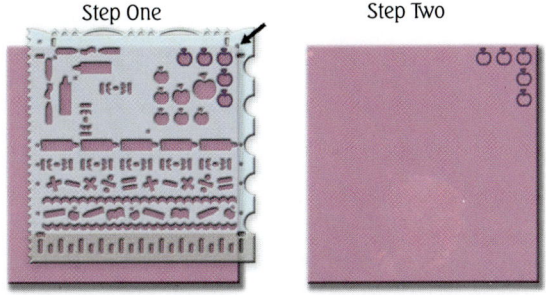

Step One	Step Two

- Position Corner Marker Hole exactly on the point of the page.
- Straighten making equal distance from each edge.

- Trace corner.
- Fill in if desired.
- Repeat in other corners.

Note - Sometimes corner(s) will layer on top of top of each other. (see page 16)

Tunnels

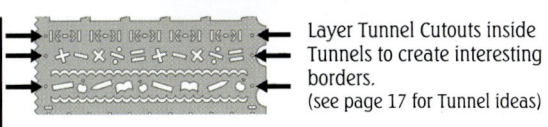

Layer Tunnel Cutouts inside Tunnels to create interesting borders.
(see page 17 for Tunnel ideas)

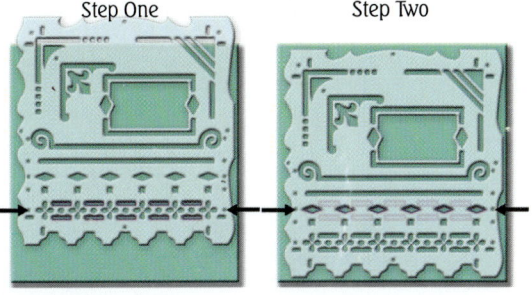

Step One	Step Two

- Position Border Buddy Tunnel Row where desired on page.
- Mark pencil dot in Marker Hole at each end of Tunnel.
- Fill in Tunnel Lines only.

- Place desired Tunnel Cutouts on page inside Tunnel matching previous pencil marks to marker holes at the end of Tunnel.
- Fill in Tunnel Cutouts.
- Erase pencil marks or doodle.

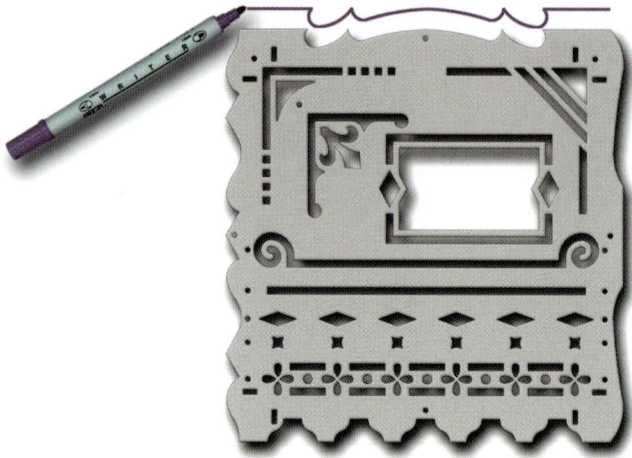

Antique Border

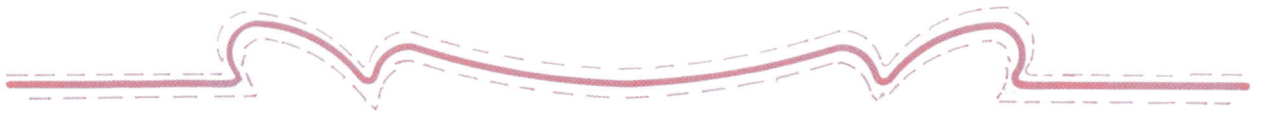

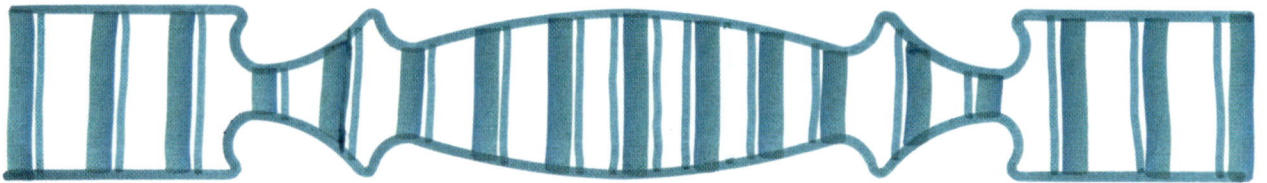

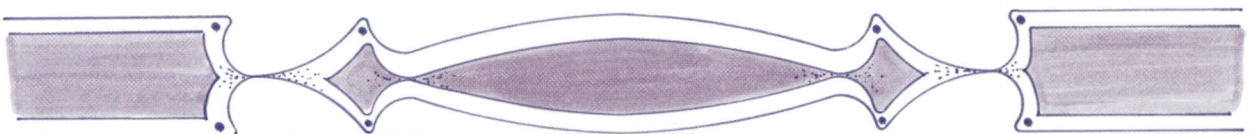

Contemporary Border

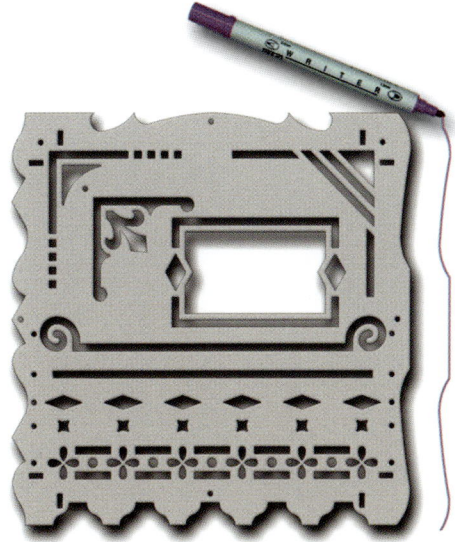

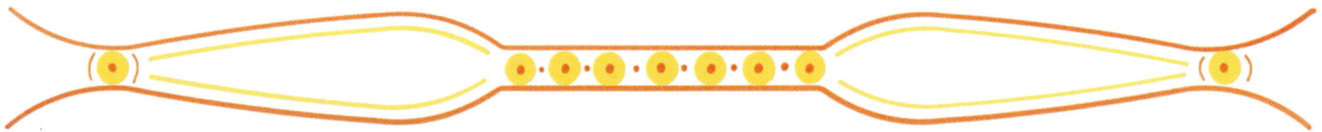

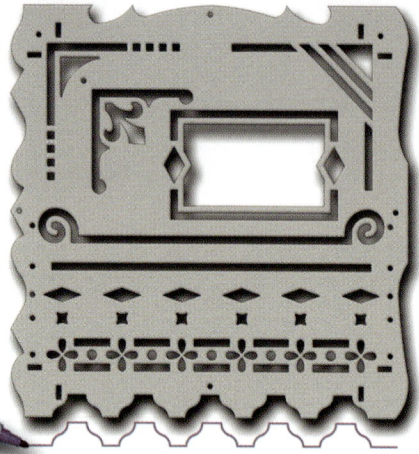

Grecian Border

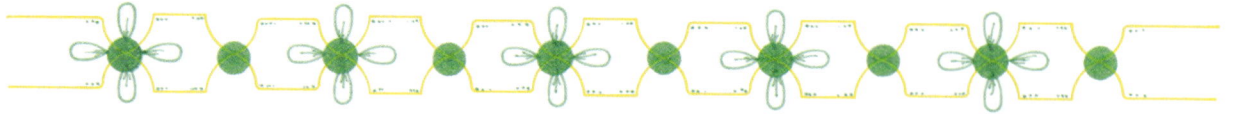

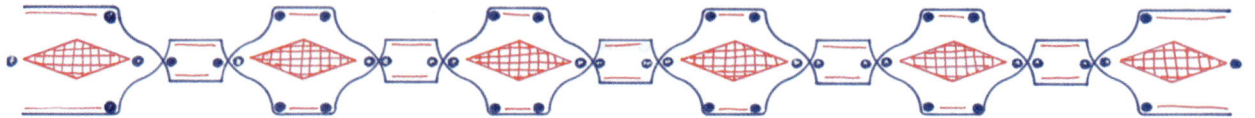

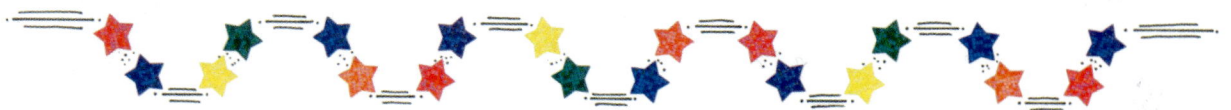

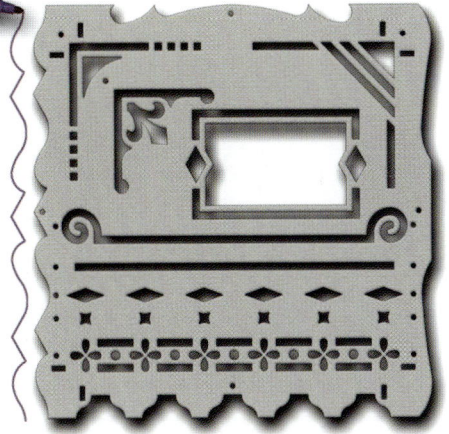

Delicate Border

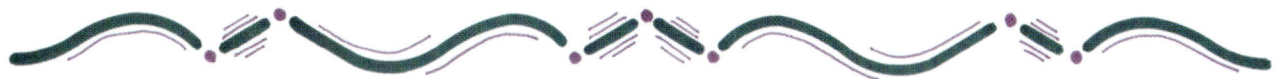

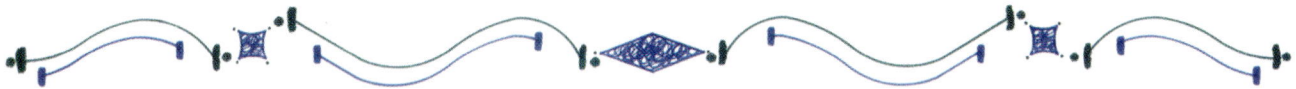

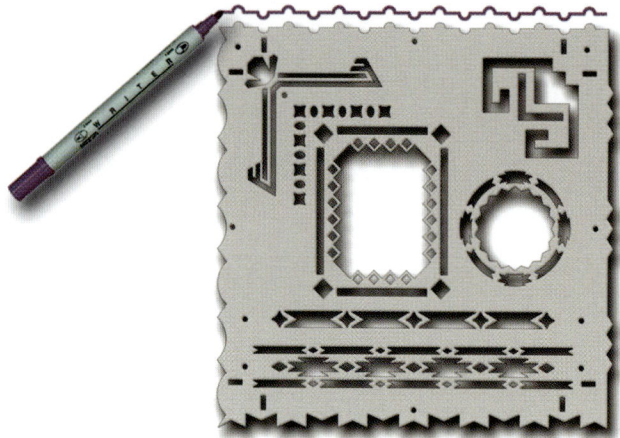

Pueblo Border

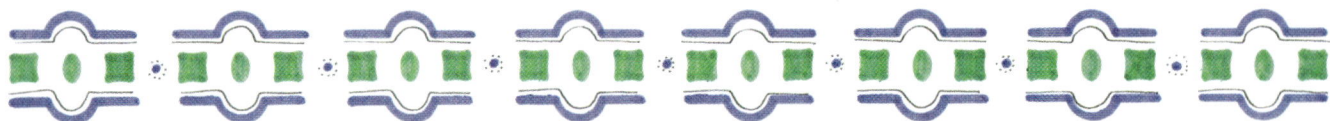

Arrowhead Border

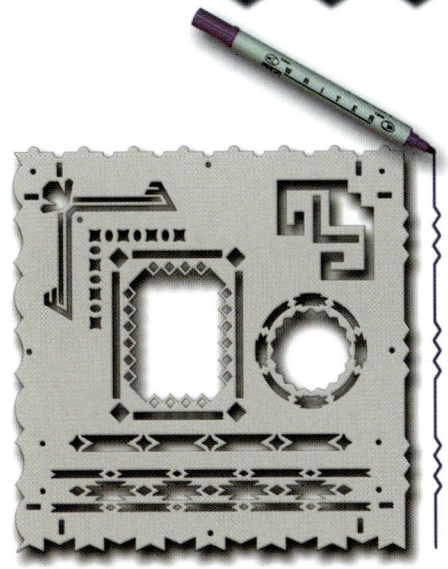

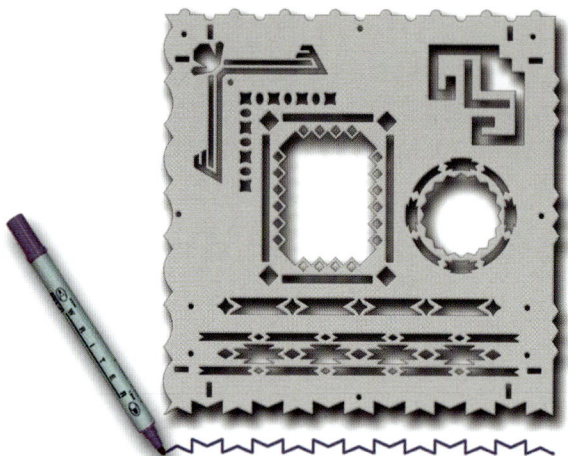

Expedition Border

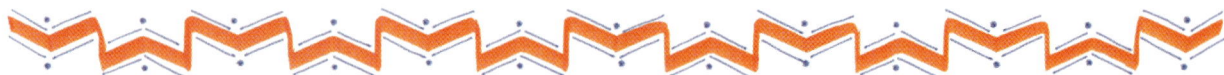

Sedona Border

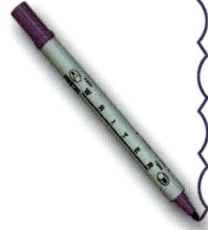

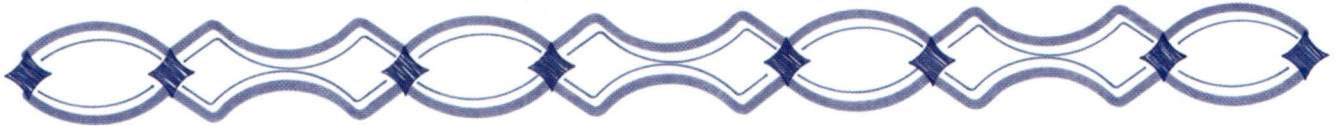

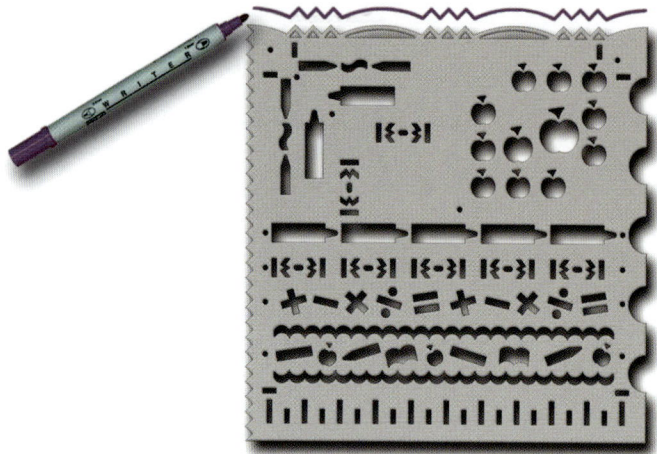

Playground Border

Postage Border

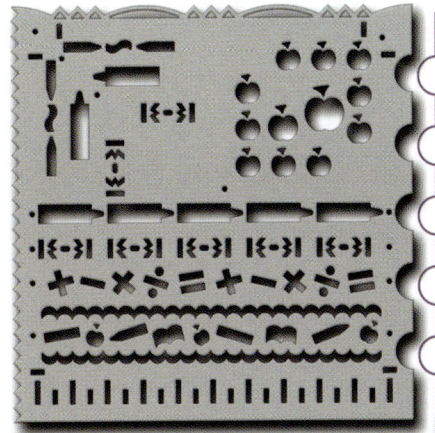

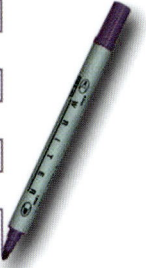

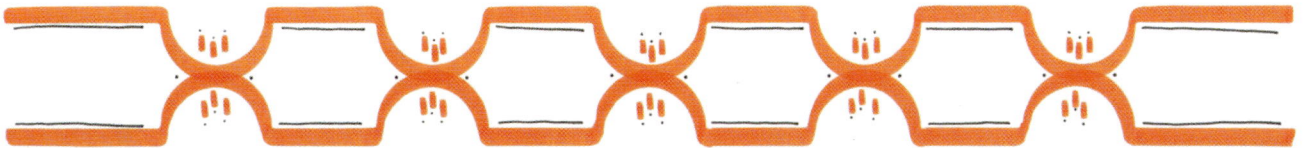

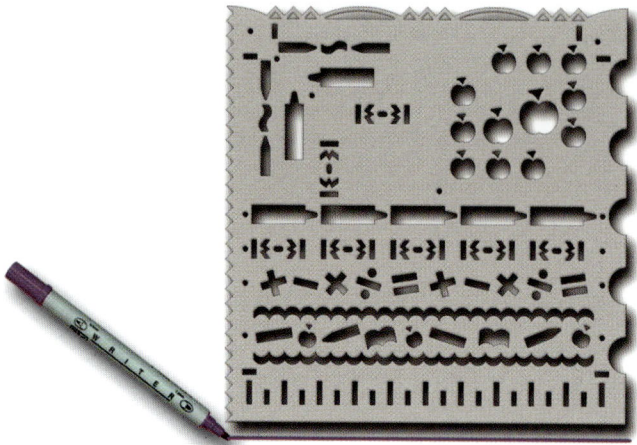

Ruler Border

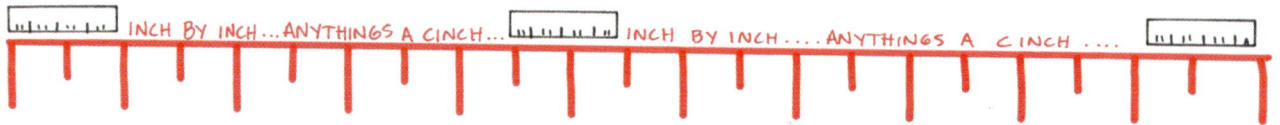

INCH BY INCH...ANYTHINGS A CINCH... INCH BY INCH....ANYTHINGS A CINCH ....

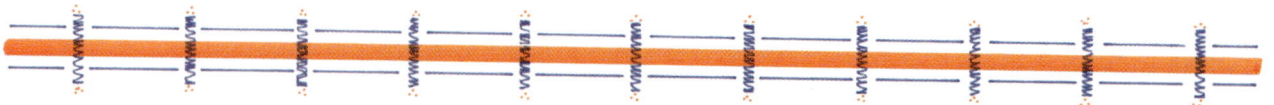

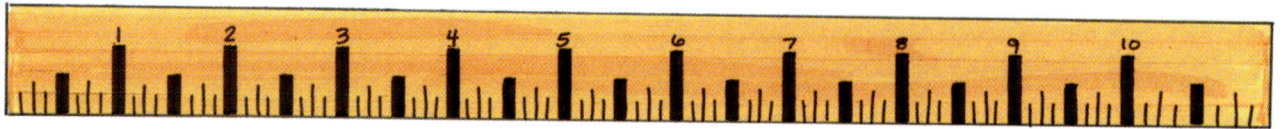

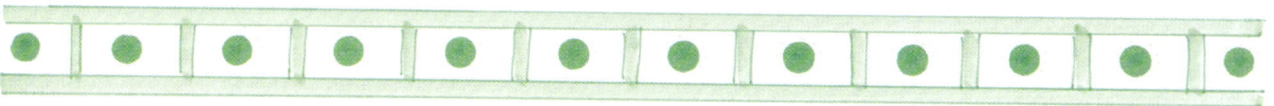

Tiny Zig Zag Border

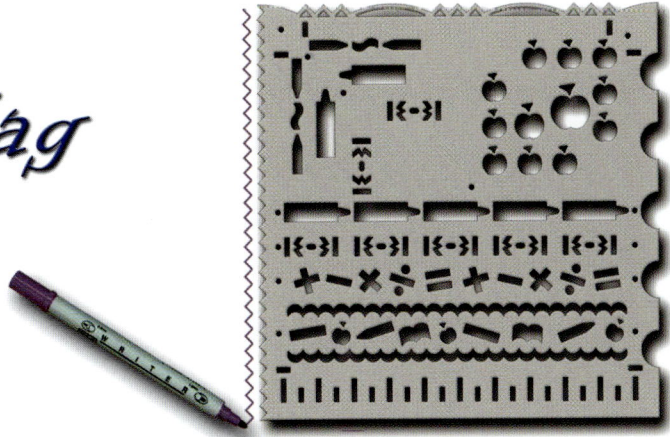

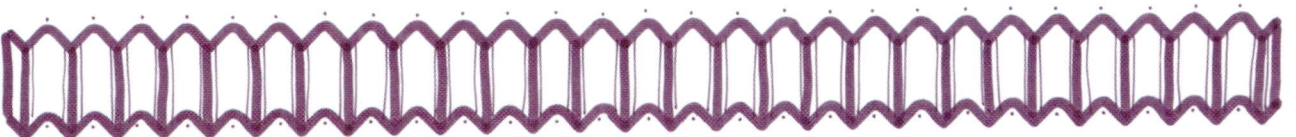

Corners & Cutouts

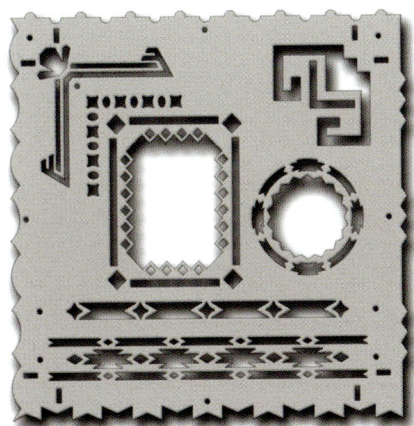

Corners & Cutouts

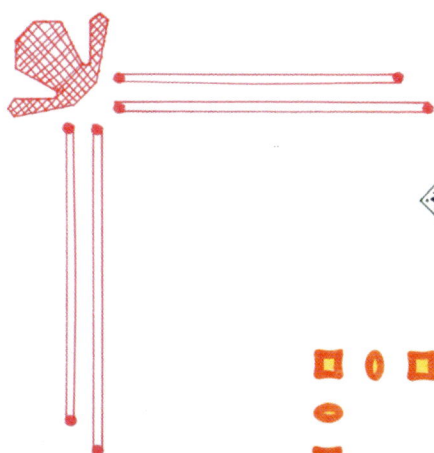

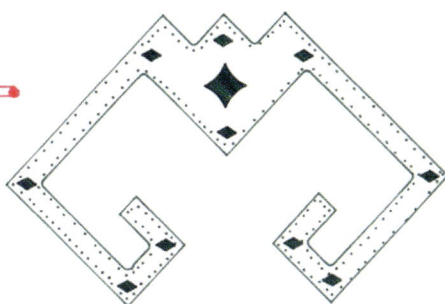

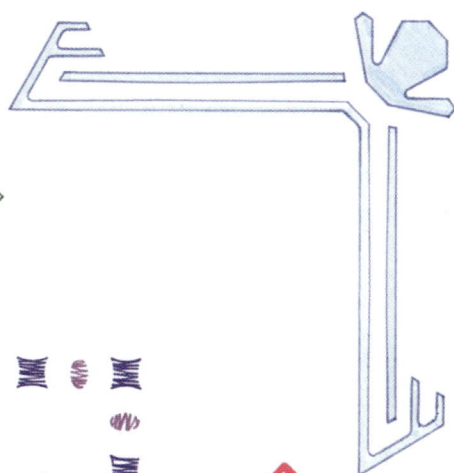

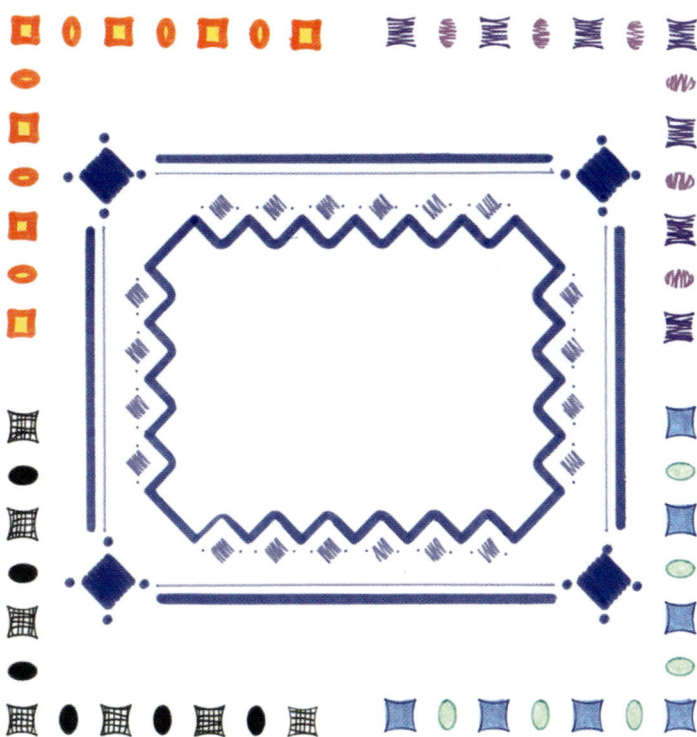

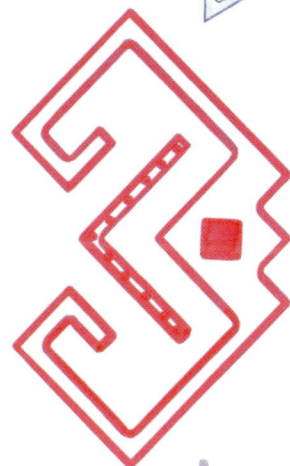

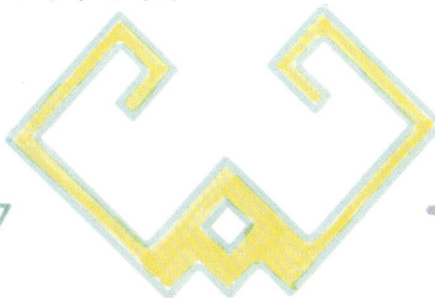

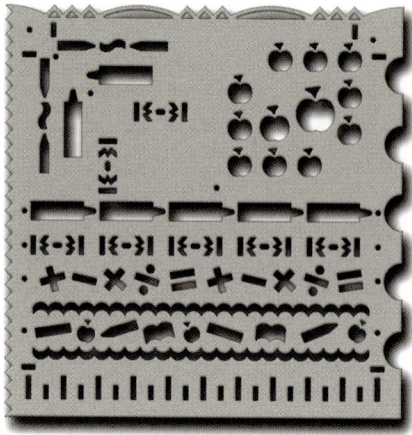

Corners & Cutouts

Tunnels & Layering

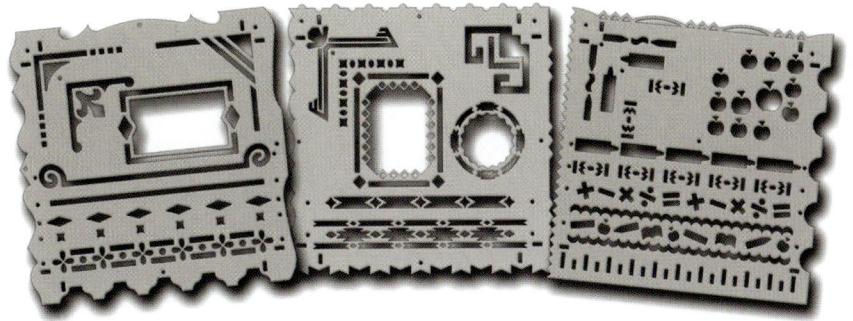

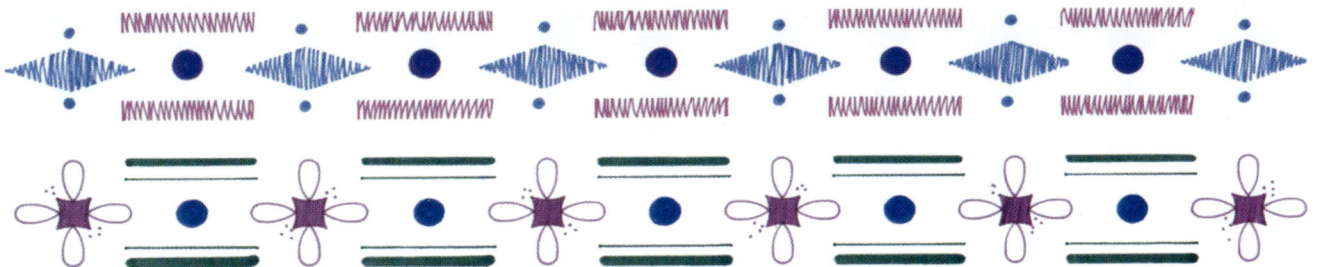

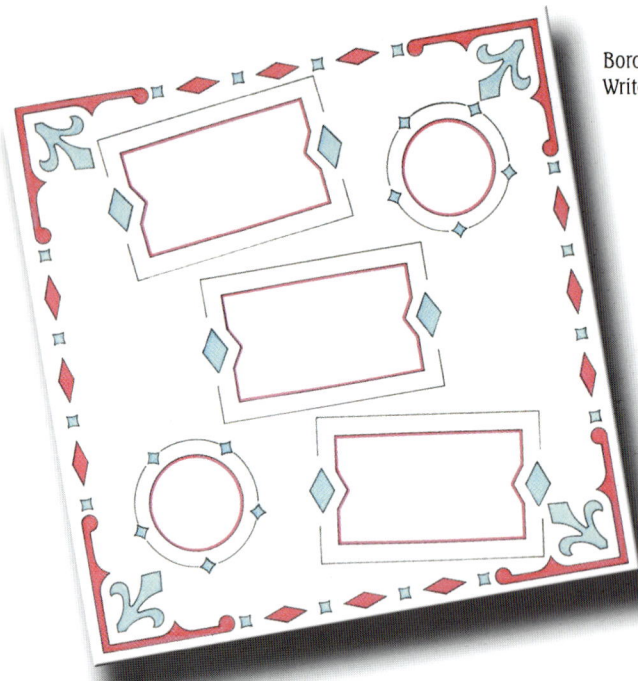

Border Buddy® – Classic
Writer™

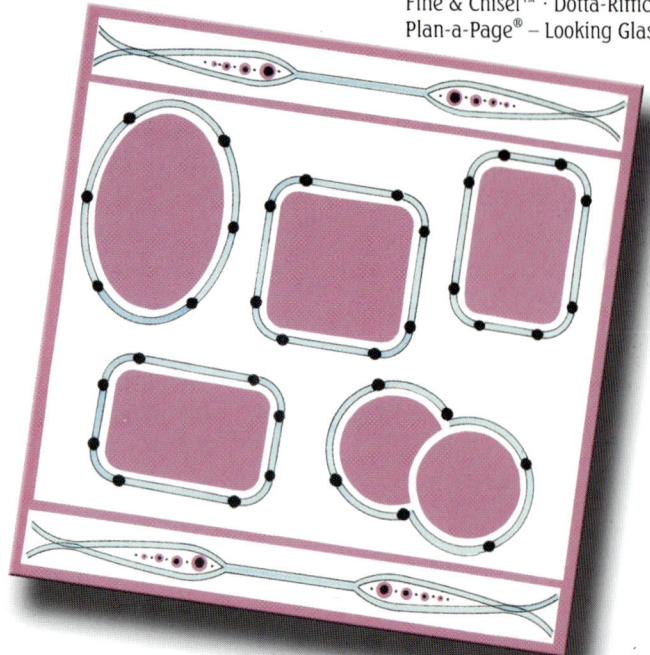

Border Buddy® – Classic
Circle Scissor™
Fine & Chisel™ · Dotta-Riffic™
Plan-a-Page® – Looking Glass

Border Buddy® – School Days
Blade Runner™
Millennium™ · Writer™ · Jel-Pop™
Stickopotamus® – Bowling Stickers
Plan-a-Page® – Tumble Down
Circle Scissor™

Border Buddy® – School Days
Stickopotamus® – Bowling Stickers
ABC Tracers™ – Block Upper
Fine & Chisel™ · Millennium™
Plan-a-Page® Jr. – Stack Up

Border Buddy® – Aztec
Blade Runner™
Plan-a-Page® Jr. – Stack Up
Stickopotamus® – School Stickers

Border Buddy® – School Days
Writer™ · Calligraphy™ · Millennium™
Plan-a-Page® – Jumble Box, Picture Window

GLENVIEW ELEMENTARY SCHOOL

Hannah 2nd grade

Back to School
Sept 1999

Flower Power!

Border Buddy® – Classic
Blade Runner™
Stickopotamus® – Daisies Stickers
Plan-a-Page® Jr. – Full Pockets
Millennium™ · Writer™

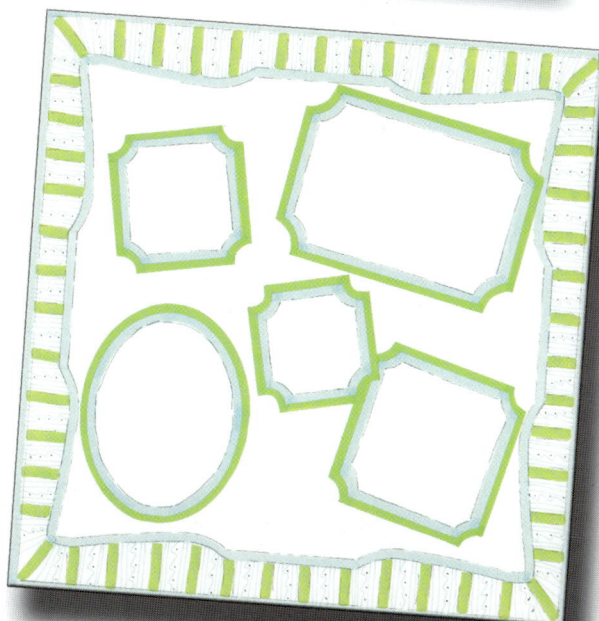

Border Buddy® – Classic
Calligraphy™ · Writer™ · Millennium™
Plan-a-Page® – Stamp Box

Border Buddy® – Aztec
Blade Runner™
Paper Shapers® – Circles
Millennium™
Moo Vue™ Film

FUN

FOR

ALL

Border Buddy® – Classic
Writer™ · Fine & Chisel™
Plan-a-Page® Jr. – Full Pockets
MM Colors by Design® – Printed Paper

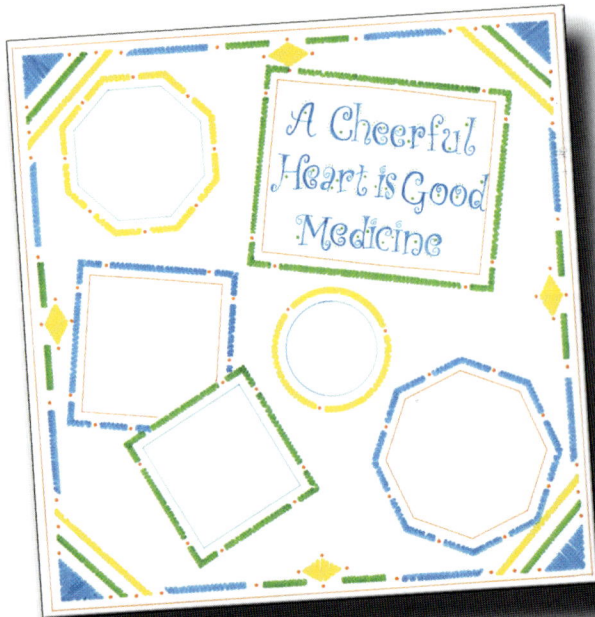

A Cheerful
Heart is Good
Medicine

Border Buddy® – Classic
Writer™
Plan-a-Page® – Tumble Down

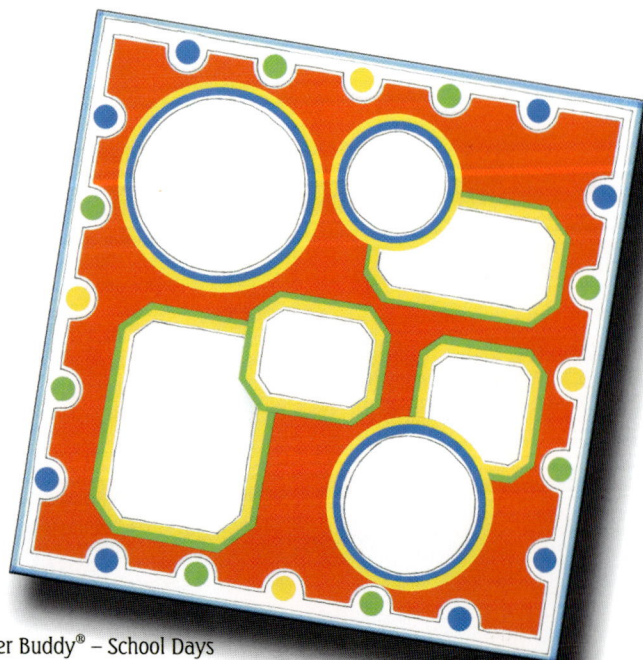

Border Buddy® – School Days
Blade Runner™
Paper Shapers® – Circles
Calligraphy™ · Millennium™
Plan-a-Page® – Cubby Hole
Circle Scissor™

Border Buddy® – School Days
Writer™ · Fine & Chisel™
Plan-a-Page® Jr. – Framework
Paper Patch® – Printed Paper

Border Buddy® – Aztec, School Days
Fine & Chisel™ · Writer™ · Dotta-Riffic™
Plan-a-Page® – Picture Window
Paper Patch® – Printed Paper

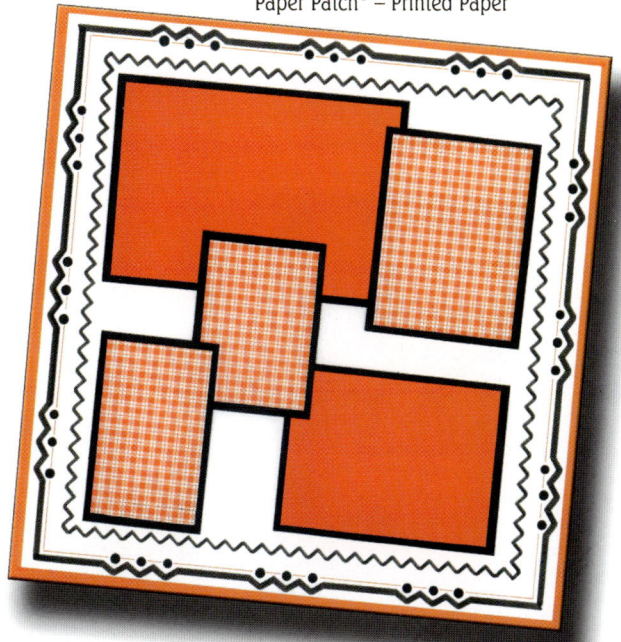

Border Buddy® – School Days
Blade Runner™
Calligraphy™ · Writer™ · Dotta-Riffic™ · Jel-Pop™
Plan-a-Page® – Looking Glass
Circle Scissor™

Carving Party

Allison & Brittany

Scrape & Scoop!

Kelsey

"Slimey"

the whole gang!

Allison

Border Buddy® – School Days
Blade Runner™
Writer™
Plan-a-Page® – Jumble Box
Over the Moon Press™ – Happy Haunting

Border Buddy® – Aztec, School Days
Blade Runner™
Scroll & Brush® · Writer™ · Millennium™

Border Buddy® – Classic, Aztec
Calligraphy™ · Opaque Writer® · Writer™
Plan-a-Page® Jr. – Full Pockets
Circle Scissor™

Border Buddy® – Aztec
Writer™

Border Buddy® – Aztec
Writer™
Plan-a-Page® Jr. – Framework

Border Buddy® – Aztec
Writer™ · Fine & Chisel™
Plan-a-Page® Jr. – Cornerstone
Provo Craft – Printed Paper

Border Buddy® – Aztec
Writer™ · Fine & Chisel™
Plan-a-Page® – Wild Cards
Sonburn – Printed Papers

Border Buddy® – Classic
Writer™ · Fine & Chisel™
Plan-a-Page® Jr. – Full Pockets
Provo Craft – Printed Paper

Border Buddy® – Classic
Writer™ – Dotta-Riffic™
Plan-a-Page® – Cubby Hole
Circle Scissor™

Border Buddy® – Classic
Blade Runner™
Writer™ · Dotta-Riffic™
Plan-a-Page® – Stamp Box
Paper Patch® – Small Plaid, Small Dots, Small Gingham

Border Buddy® – Aztec
Fine & Chisel™
Plan-a-Page® Jr. – Cornerstone

Border Buddy® – Classic
Writer™
Blade Runner™
Plan-a-Page® – Storyboard

Border Buddy® – Aztec
Writer™
Plan-a-Page® – Jumble box

Border Buddy® – Classic
Blade Runner™
Writer™
Paper Patch® – Printed Paper
Paper Shapers® – Diamond, Circle

Border Buddy® – Classic
Writer™ · Calligraphy™
Plan-a-Page® – Picture Window

You Color my World

Border Buddy® – School Days
Writer™ · Fine & Chisel™

25

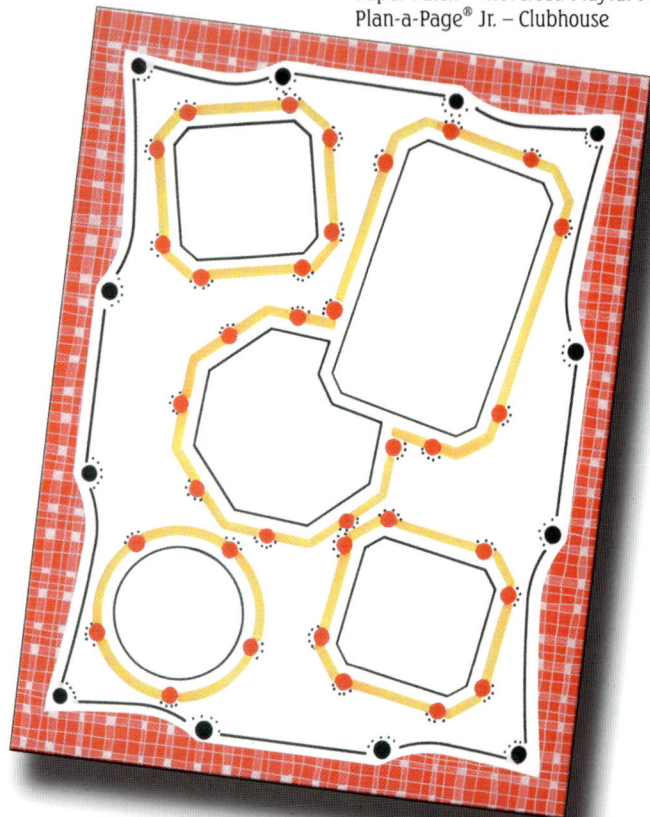

Border Buddy® – School Days, Aztec
Writer™
Blade Runner™
ABC Tracers™ – School Days Lower and Upper

Border Buddy® – Classic
Blade Runner™
Fine & Chisel™ · Dotta-Riffic™
Paper Patch® - Reversed Playful Plai
Plan-a-Page® Jr. – Clubhouse

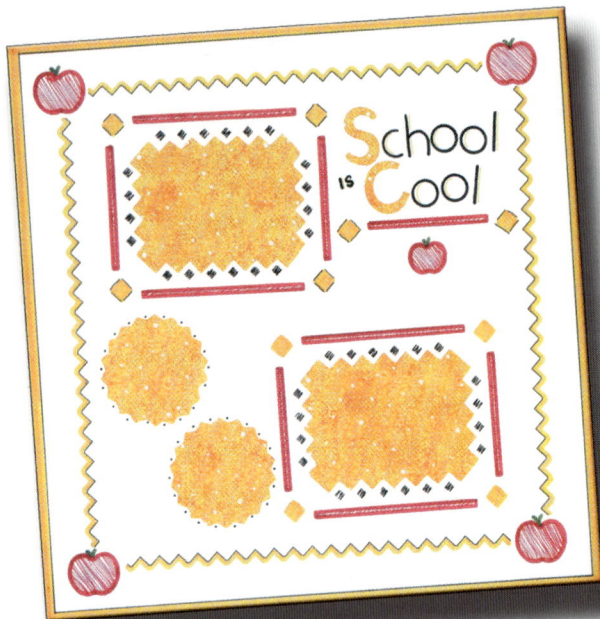

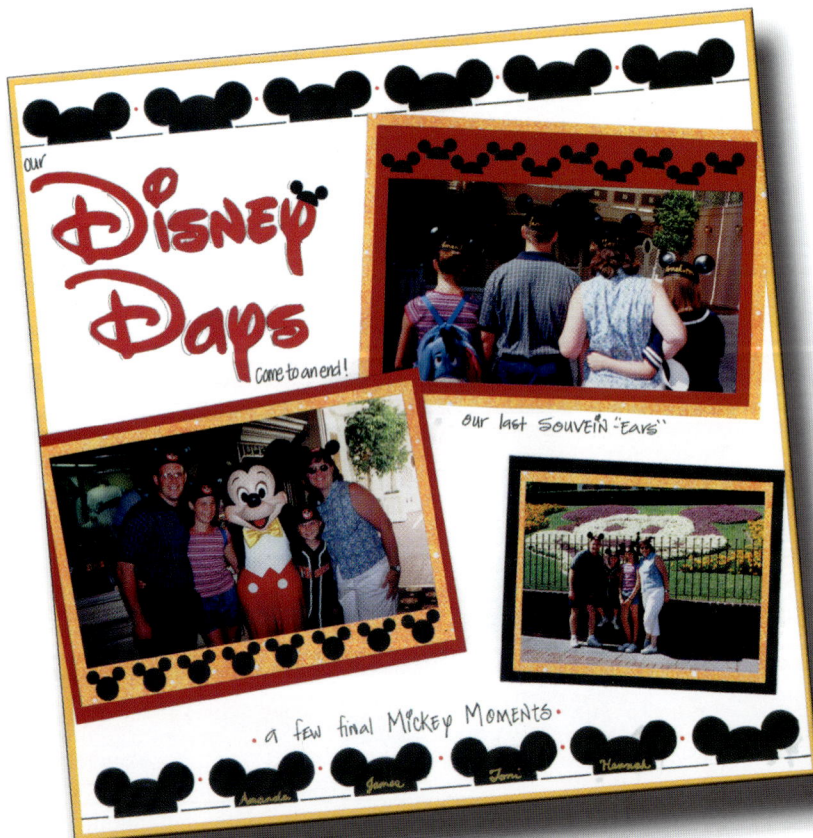

Border Buddy® – School Days
Writer™ · Millennium™
©Disney Mickey Punch
Plan-a-Page® – Picture Window

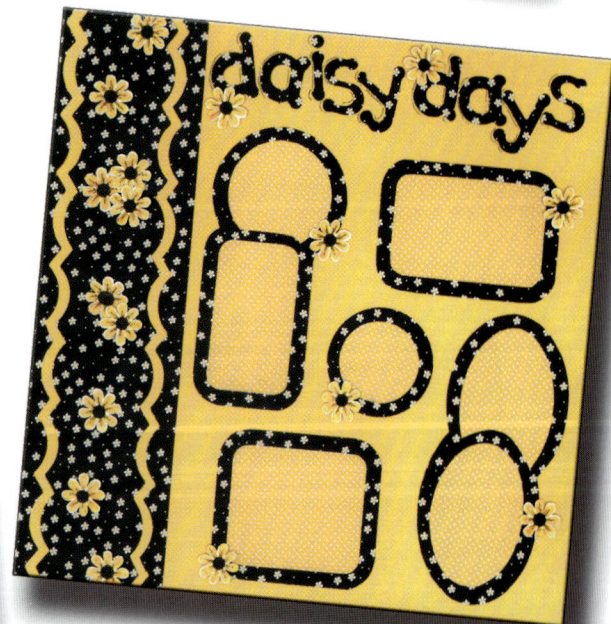

Border Buddy® – Aztec, Classic
Blade Runner™
Paper Patch® – Printed Papers
ABC Tracers™ – Dot Lower
Writer™ · Millennium™
Plan-a-Page® Jr. – Cameo Pictures
Circle Scissor™

BACK TO SCHOOL

Wesley-
4th grade

Taylor-
5th grade

Allison- kindergarten

Kelsey-
2nd grade

We're on our way!

Freedom!

the
"happy" group...

the
"not-happy" group!

STOP

Border Buddy® – School Days
ABC Tracers™ – Block Upper
Blade Runner™
Millennium™ · Memory Pencils™
Plan-a-Page® – Cubby Hole
Circle Scissor™

Border Buddy® – School Days
Writer™
Plan-a-Page® Jr. – Slide Show
Paper Patch® – White Dots on Black

Give them
an inch and
they think
they're the
RULER!

Border Buddy® – School Days
Fine & Chisel™ · Writer™
Blade Runner™
Plan-a-Page® – Stamp Box
Circle Scissor™
Paper Patch® – Printed Paper

school
days

Border Buddy® – School Days
Calligraphy™ · Writer™
Plan-a-Page® Jr. – Full Pockets
Circle Scissor™

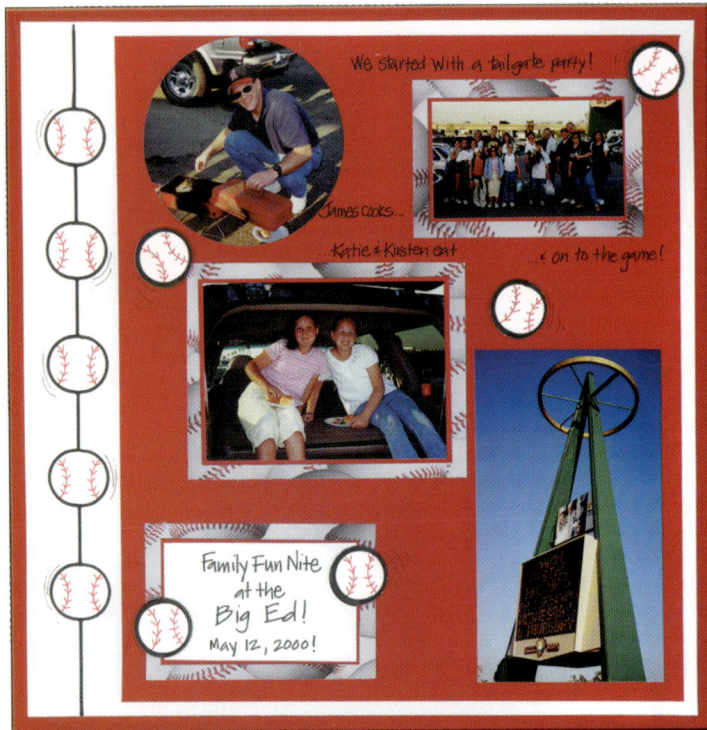

We started with a tailgate party!

James cooks...

...Kathie & Kristen eat

...on to the game!

Family Fun Nite
at the
Big Ed!
May 12, 2000!

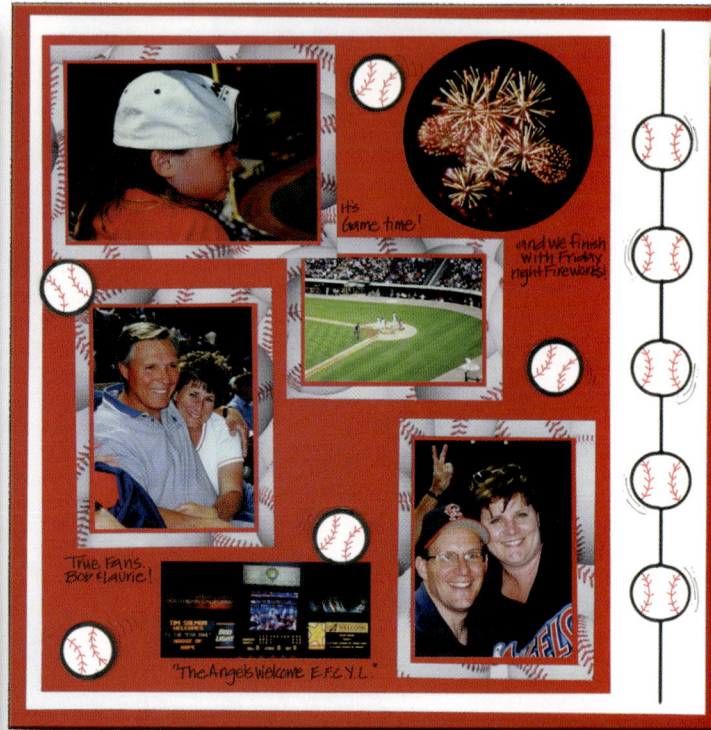

Its
Game time!

...and we finish
with Friday
night Fireworks!

True Fans.
Bob & Laurie!

"The Angels Welcome E.F.C.Y.L."

Border Buddy® – School Days
Writer™ · Millennium™
Circle Scissor™
Plan-a-Page® – Picture Window
FMI Inc. – Baseball Paper

Border Buddy® – Classic
Blade Runner™
Paper Patch® – Reversed Playful Plaid Paper
Opaque Writer®
Plan-a-Page® – Jumble box

you
stole
my heart

Border Buddy® – Aztec
Fine & Chisel™
Paper Shapers® – Folk Heart
Plan-a-Page® – Tumble Down

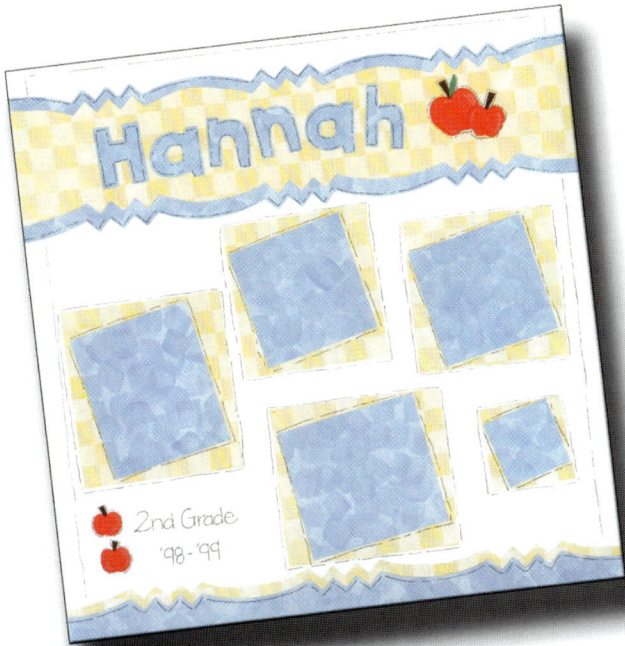

Border Buddy® – School Days
Blade Runner™
Millennium™ · Memory Pencils™
Provo Craft – Printed Papers

Border Buddy® – School Days
Writer™
Plan-a-Page® Jr. – Clubhouse

Border Buddy® – School Days
Blade Runner™
Calligraphy™ · Millennium™
Over the Moon Press™ – Classroom Dots
Paper Patch® – Printed Paper
ABC Tracers™ -School Days Lower
Plan-a-Page® Jr. -Full Pockets

Border Buddy® – School Days
Writer™ · Millennium™

Border Buddy® – Classic
Blade Runner™
Writer™ · Photo Twin™
Paper Patch® · Sonburn · MM Colors by Design® – Printed Papers
Moo Vue™ Film

Border Buddy® – Classic
Blade Runner™
Writer™
Frances Meyer – Printed Paper
Plan-a-Page® – Jumble box

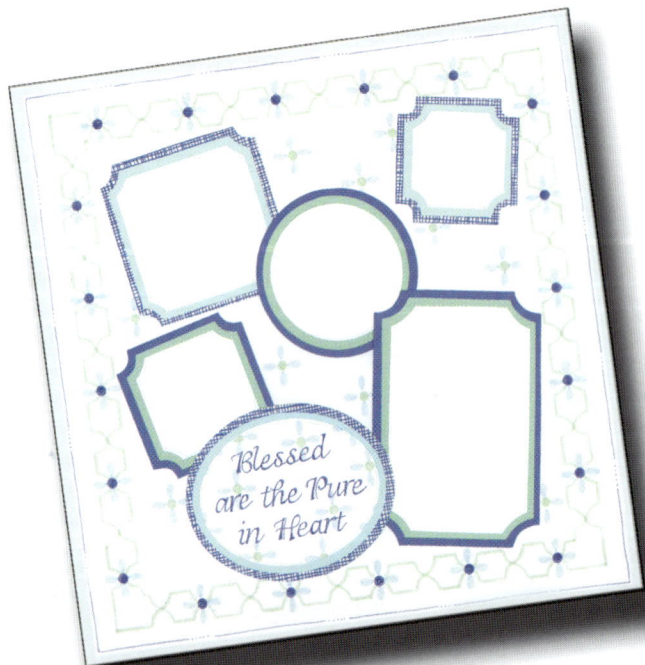

Border Buddy® – Classic
Writer™
Plan-a-Page® – Stamp Box

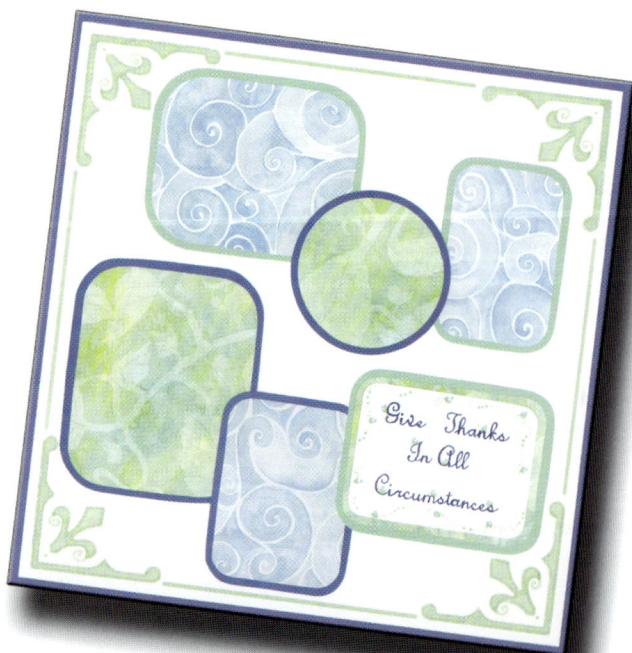

Border Buddy® – Classic
Writer™ · Calligraphy™
Sonburn · MM Colors by Design® – Printed Papers

Border Buddy® – Classic
Blade Runner™
Writer™ · Scroll & Brush® · Jel-Pop™
Plan-a-Page® Jr. – Cameo Pictures
MM Colors by Design® – Printed Papers

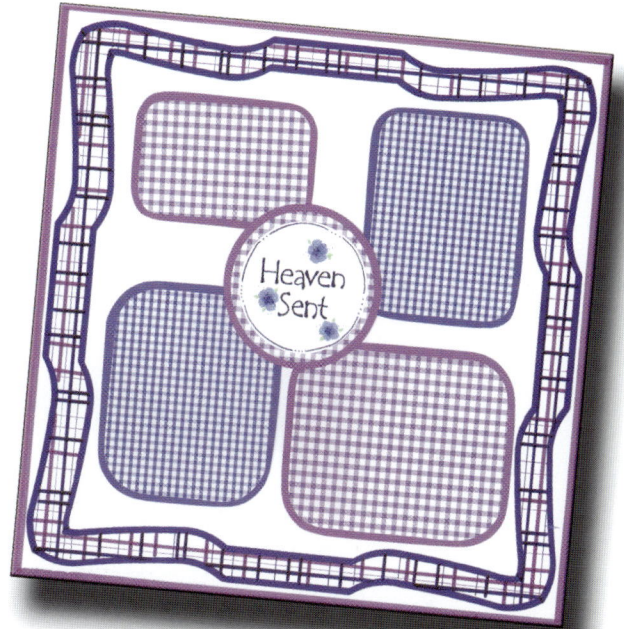

You Are Special

Heaven Sent

Border Buddy® – Classic
Writer™ · Fine & Chisel™ · Scroll & Brush®
Plan-a-Page® – Storyboard
Paper Patch® · Frances Meyer – Printed Papers

Count Your Blessings

Border Buddy® – Classic
Writer™ · Calligraphy™
Plan-a-Page® – Picture Window

Brotherly Love

Wesley

Taylor

Border Buddy® – Classic
Blade Runner™
Writer™ · Fine & Chisel™ · Calligraphy™
Hot Off The Press – Printed Paper

31

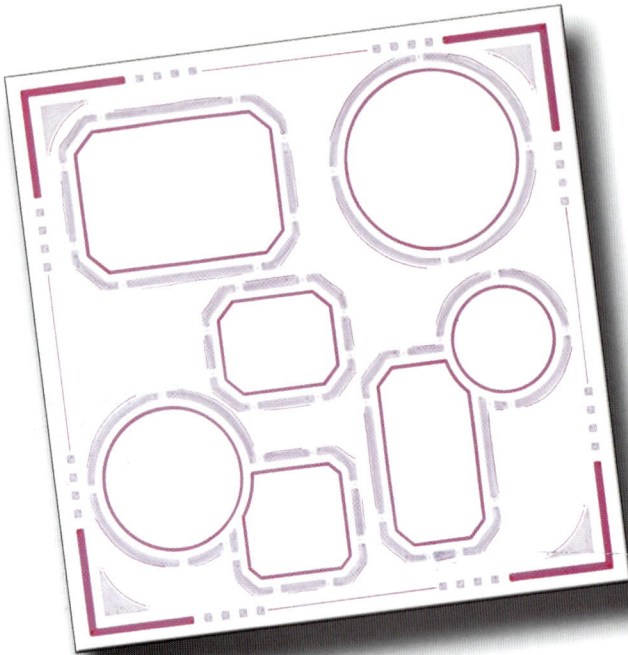

Border Buddy® – Classic
Writer™
Plan-a-Page® – Cubby Hole

It's a

G
I
R
L

Border Buddy® – Classic
Blade Runner™
©Susan Branch, MM Colors by Design® – Printed Papers
Millennium™
Plan-a-Page® – Cubby Hole
Circle Scissor™

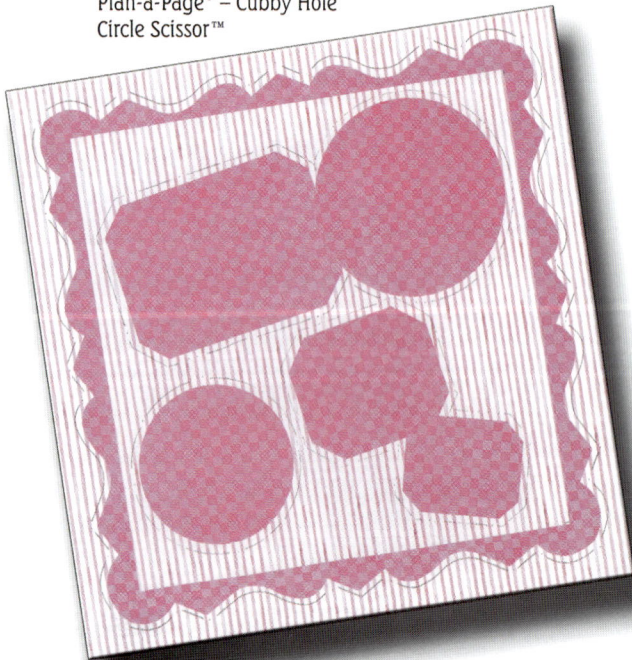

CURLY GIRL

Hannah tries out the new curlers

Border Buddy® – Aztec
Writer™ · Calligraphy™
ABC Tracers™ – Dot Upper
Plan-a-Page® – Wild Cards
Paper Patch® – Printed Paper

June 2000

Beautiful Ballerinas

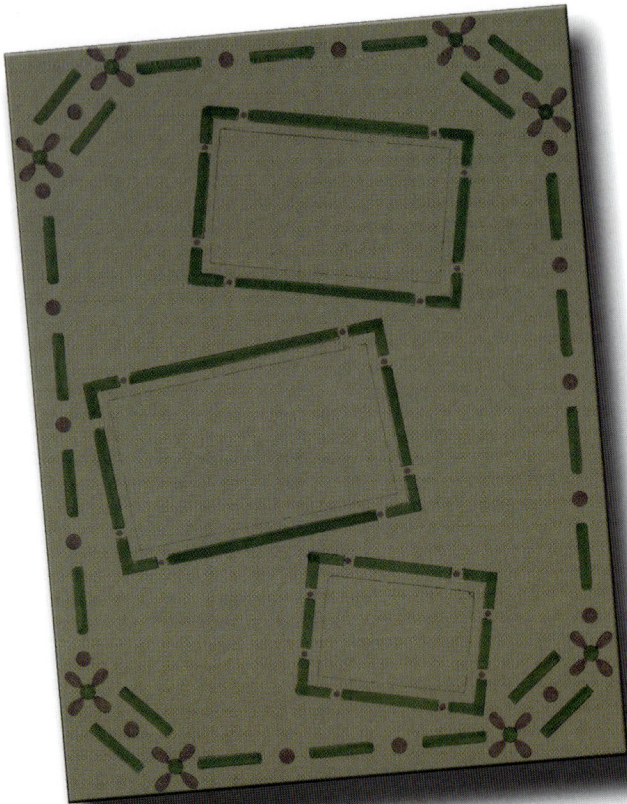

Border Buddy® – Classic
Writer™ · Millennium™
Plan-a-Page® Jr. – Slide Show

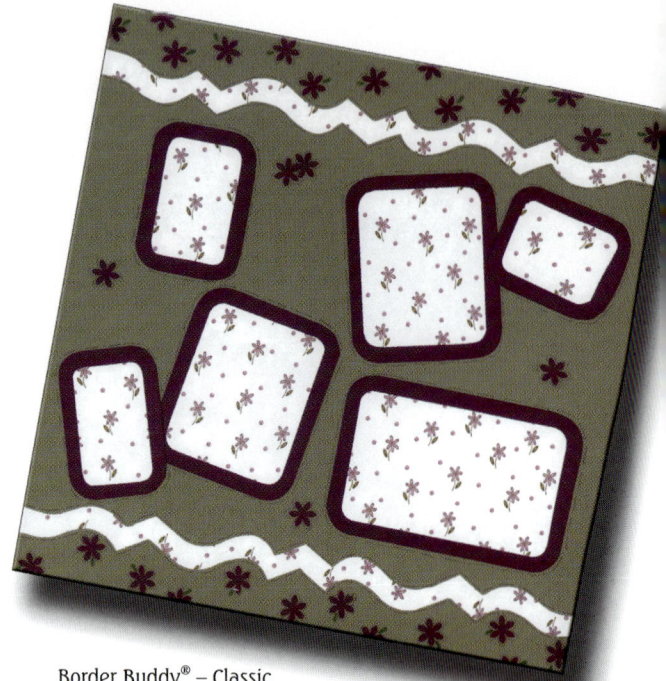

Border Buddy® – Classic
Blade Runner™
Writer™ · Scroll & Brush®
Paper Shapers® – Daisy
Plan-a-Page® Jr. – Balancing Act
Over The Moon Press – Sweet Violets and Dots

Border Buddy® – Classic
Blade Runner™
Paper Shapers® – Daisy
Over the Moon Press™ – Sweet Violets and Dots
Writer™ · Photo Twin™
Plan-a-Page® – Tumble Down
Circle Scissor™

Border Buddy® – Classic
Blade Runner™
Over the Moon Press™ – Sweet Violets and Checks
Opaque Writer®
Circle Scissor™

34

Border Buddy® – School Days
Scroll & Brush® · Writer™ · Jel-Pop™
Plan-a-Page® – Tumble Down

Border Buddy® – Classic, School Days
Blade Runner™
Scroll & Brush® · Writer™ · Jel-Pop™

Border Buddy® – Classic, School Days
Blade Runner™
Writer™ · Jel-Pop™
Plan-a-Page® – Wild Cards

Border Buddy® – Aztec
Calligraphy™ · Writer™ · Dotta-Riffic™
Plan-a-Page® – Tumble Down

SUMMER SUN — Smiles · Surf

SUMMER FUN — football

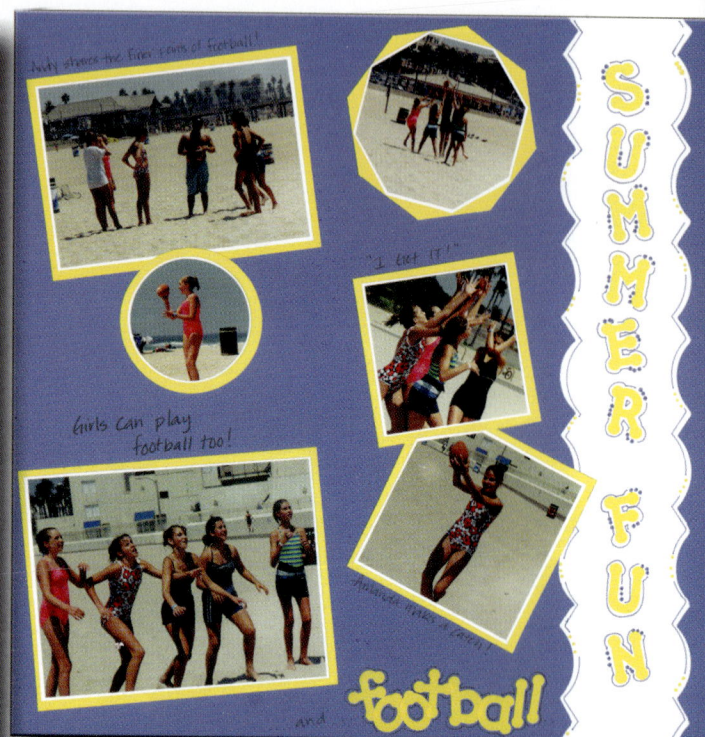

Border Buddy® – Aztec
Blade Runner™
Writer™
Stickopotamus® - Dot Alphabet Stickers
Plan-a-Page® – Tumble Down
Circle Scissor™

Border Buddy® – Classic, Aztec
Writer™
Plan-a-Page® – Picture Window

Border Buddy® – Aztec
Writer™ · Dotta-Riffic™ · Fine & Chisel
Plan-a-Page® Jr. – Balancing Act